My First Book of Prayers

Mi Primer Libro de Oraciones

My First Book of Prayers

Mi Primer Libro de Oraciones

Illustrated by
Stephanie McFetridge Britt

ideals children's books
Nashville, Tennessee

ISBN-13: 978-0-8249-5447-5

ISBN-10: 0-8249-5447-5

Published by Ideals Children's Books

An imprint of Ideals Publications

A Guideposts Company

Nashville, Tennessee

www.idealsbooks.com

Copyright © 2002 by Ideals Publications

Illustrations copyright © 2001

by Stephanie McFetridge Britt

Printed and bound in Mexico by R.R. Donnelley

Library of Congress CIP data on file

Cover design by Marisa Calvin

Book design by Jenny Eber Hancock

3 5 7 9 10 8 6 4

For Sarah

To Parents and Teachers:

My First Book of Prayers, Mi Primer Libro de Oraciones, is one of a series of bilingual books specially created by Ideals Children's Books to help children and their parents learn to read both Spanish and English.

If the child's first language is English, he or she will understand and be able to read the text on the left-hand pages of this book. If the child wishes to read Spanish, he or she will be able to read the right-hand pages of the book. Whether the child's native language is English or Spanish, he or she will be able to compare the text of the two pages and, thus, learn to read both English and Spanish.

Also included at the end of the story are several common words listed in both English and Spanish that the child may review. These include both nouns, with their gender in Spanish, and verbs. In the case of the verbs, the Spanish verbs have the endings that indicate their use in the story.

Parents and teachers will want to use this book as a beginning reader for children who speak either English or Spanish.

A los Padres y los Maestros:

My First Book of Prayers, Mi Primer Libro de Oraciones, es parte de una serie de libros bilingüe hecho especialmente por Ideals Children's Books para ayudar a los niños y a sus padres a aprender como leer en Español e Inglés.

Si el primer idioma del niño es Inglés, él puede leer y entender lo que está escrito en la página a la izquierda. Si el niño quiere leer en Español, él puede leer las páginas a la derecha. Cualquiera que sea el idioma nativo, el Inglés o el Español, el niño podrá comparar lo escrito en las dos páginas y entonces aprenderá como leer en Inglés y en Español.

Al final de la historia hay una lista de vocabulario con palabras comunes en Inglés y en Español. La lista tiene ambos sustantivos, con el género y verbos en Español con los fines que indican el uso en la historia.

Los padres y los maestros desearán usar este libro como nivel inicial de lectura para niños que hablan Inglés o Español.

Lord, teach a

little child

to pray,

and, oh, accept

my prayer;

I know You hear

the words I say,

for You

are everywhere.

Author Unknown

Señor, enséñame

a orar,

Y acepta mi oración;

Yo sé que Tú

me oyes,

Pues estás en

todo lugar.

Autor Desconocido

Thank You

for the fish

that swim;

I really like to

look at them.

Thank You

for the birds

that sing.

Thank You,

Lord,

for everything.

Author Unknown

Gracias por peces

que nadan;

Tanto me encanta

mirarlos.

Gracias por aves

que cantan.

Por todo Te

doy las gracias.

Autor Desconocido

For flowers that

bloom about

our feet,

For tender

grass, so fresh

and sweet,

For song of

bird and hum of

bee, Father in

heaven,

we thank Thee!

Por las flores

que florecen

a mis pies,

Por la hierba, tan

fresca y bella,

Por el canto del

pájaro y zumbido

de abeja,

Padre celestial,

Te damos gracias!

For blue of stream,

for blue of sky,

For pleasant

shade of

branches high,

For beauty of the

blowing trees,

Father in heaven,

we thank Thee!

Por el azul del

agua y del cielo,

Por la sombra agradable

de ramas altas,

Por la belleza del viento

entre los árboles,

Padre celestial, Te

damos gracias!

For mother love

and father care,

For brothers

strong and

sisters fair,

Father in heaven,

we thank Thee!

Ralph Waldo Emerson

Por el amor de
madre y el cuidar
de padre,
Por hermanos
fuertes y
hermanas lindas,
Padre celestial,
Te damos gracias!

Ralph Waldo Emerson

For each new

morning and its light,

For rest and shelter

of the night,

For every gift Your

goodness sends,

We thank You,

loving God.

Author Unknown

Por la luz de cada

amanecer,

Por el descanso y

abrigo de cada

noche,

Por cada dádiva

que Tu bondad

nos presta,

Te damos gracias,

Dios amoroso.

Autor Desconocido

Heavenly Father,

hear my prayer;

Keep me in

Thy loving care.

Guide me through

each lovely day,

In my work

and in my play.

Keep me pure

and sweet and true

In everything

I say and do.

Abbie Burr

Padre celestial, oye

mi oración;

Guárdame con Tu

amor bondadoso.

Guíame a través de

cada día hermoso,

En mi trabajo

y en mi jugar.

En todo lo

que digo y hago

Guárdame puro,

amable y fiel.

Abbie Burr

We thank You, Lord,

For birds

and flowers,

For trees

and winds,

And gentle

showers.

Te damos gracias,

Señor,

Por pájaros y flores,

Por árboles y brisas,

Y lluvias ligeras.

We thank You for

Our clothes

and food,

For friends

and parents,

Kind and good.

Herbert Stoneley

Te damos gracias
Por ropa y comida,
Por amigos y padres,
Buenos y amables.

Herbert Stoneley

Father, we thank
You for the night
And for the
pleasant
morning light,
For rest and food
and loving care
And all that makes
the day so fair.

Author Unknown

Padre, Te damos

gracias por la noche

Y por la luz

del amanecer,

Por el descanso

y la comida

Y la hermosura

de cada día.

Autor Desconocido

I see the moon

and the moon

sees me.

God bless

the moon

and God bless me.

Author Unknown

Yo veo la luna

La luna me ve a mí.

Dios bendice

la luna

Y Dios me bendice.

Autor Desconocido

Now I lay me

down to sleep.

I pray the Lord

my soul to keep.

Watch over me

throughout

the night

And bring me safe

to morning light.

Author Unknown

Ya me acuesto

para dormir.

Te pido, Señor,

mi alma guardar.

Cuídame por

toda la noche

Y traeme seguro

al amanecer.

Autor Desconocido

Vocabulary words used in

My First Book of Prayers
Mi Primer Libro de Oraciones

English	Spanish	English	Spanish
my	mi	I like	me encanta
first	primer	to look at	mirar
book	el libro	birds	las aves
prayers	las oraciones	they sing	cantan
Lord	Señor	I give	doy
teach me	enséñame	flowers	las flores
to pray	orar	they bloom	florecen
accept	acepta	feet	los pies
I know	yo sé	grass	la hierba
you hear	oyes	fresh	fresca
you are	estás	lovely	bella
everywhere	en todo lugar	song	el canto
thank you	gracias	buzz (n.)	el zumbido
for	por	bees	las abejas
fish	los peces	heavenly	celestial
that	que	blue	el azul
they swim	nadan	water	la agua
so much	tanto	sky	el cielo